Plant Based Trail Meals

TERRA EDITION

Fast, easy and tasty
trail-tested recipes for
any outdoor activity

It's not always about the destination...but sometimes nature provides.

Ruby Mountain
-North Cascades National Park, WA

by Chef Corso
& the Outdoor Eats community

Thanks for coming along!

Our mission at Outdoor Eats is to get folks excited about cooking outside.

Every recipe is trail-tested by a member of our community and

– uses 10 ingredients or less
– is ready in 30 min or less
– weighs as little as 4 oz per serving
– requires no pre-prep and no dehydrating
– uses fresh, real ingredients
– is amazingly tasty!

We hope these meals elevate your experience and fuel you on your next epic thru-hike or Sunday stroll.

Get outside
Eat well
Share the tasty experience

Introduction

How to use this cookbook

Thanks for bringing Outdoor Eats along on your trek!

We believe you can make amazing meals anywhere with any camp stove.

The recipes are formatted for smaller capacity hiking stoves. They are created to be easy to shop for and fast to cook up. All ingredients should be available at most grocery stores (unless noted on the recipe).

Plant based eating on the trail can be a challenging. We know every belly is different and you have your specific list of ingredients you eat or don't eat. **You can use the recipes as a guide** or go off-recipe to create your own tasty creation. Enjoy dairy/cheese? Eat eggs or fish? Go nuts! Let us know what you create!

Need to feed more people?
Just increase the recipe quantities and batch cook it as needed.

Have extra?
Share with a new hiking buddy!

Need other recipe ideas?
@outdooreats365
www.outdooreats.com
YouTube: Chef Corso

Contents

Become a
recipe tester!

Join the Outdoor Eats community.

What does that mean?
– Receive a NEW recipe from Chef Corso.
– Take it outside.
– Test it.
– Take a couple photos.
– Share feedback.

Chef Corso edits and shares with the whole community!

Visit
www.outdooreats.com

The Plant Based Pantry

The Plant Based Pantry

Tasty, filling and packable ingredients!

Carbs

Instant Rice
Instant Mashed Potatoes
Instant Sweet Potatoes
Instant Cous Cous
Rice Noodles
Ramen Noodles
Grits/Polenta/Corn Meal/Masa
Pre-cooked Grain Mixes
Quinoa
Stuffing Mix
Pasta (*stick with thin or small shapes for fastest cooking*)
Tortillas (*Flour, Corn, GF*)
Bread/Rolls
Bagels
Crackers

Protein

Nuts/Seeds
Peanut/Nut Butter & Powder
Packaged Jack Fruit
Veggie Jerky (*hydrates surprisingly well in soups*)
Pre-cooked/Packaged Tofu
JUST Egg® Products
Chia Seeds
Tempeh
Seitan
Edamame
Peas
Mung Beans
Freeze-dried Legumes
Chickpeas, Lentils, Pinto, and Black Beans
Spirulina
Hemp Hearts
Boca Burgers®
Morningstar Farms® Products
Field Roast® Products
Soyrizo®
Textured Vegetable Protein (TVP)
Alternative Meat Options

Veggies

Snap Peas
Wasabi Peas
Avocados
Olives
Carrots, shredded/coins
Cauliflower/Cauli Rice
Broccoli/Broccoli Rice
Kale/Dark Leafy Greens
Green Onions
French's Fried Onions
Shallots
Bell Peppers
Zucchini/Yellow Squash
Baby Tomatoes
Mushrooms (fresh or dried)
Brussels Sprouts
Green Beans

Flavor

Spice Mixes
Salsa Packets
Gravy Mixes
Asian Sauces
Hot Sauce
Condiment Packets
Soy Sauce Powder
Lemon/Lime
Vinegars (*apple cider, black, balsamic, red wine, rice*)
Dried Fruit
Sesame Oil
Coconut Oil
Coconut Shavings
Coconut Milk Powder
Coconut Water Powder

Don't Forget

Instant Coffee/Tea
Electrolyte Tabs/Packets
Trail Bars
Other Desserts
    UNREAL®, OCHO®, Hu® or
    The Ginger People® candies

**Morningstar
Breakfast Muffins**
Seattle, WA

**Avocado, Tomato, Spinach
Breakfast Sandwiches**
Seattle, WA

Soyrizo Brekkie Burritos
Mt. Baker, WA

**AAAlmond,
Apricot Oatmeal**
North Cascades NP - WA

Breakfast

UW Arboretum
-Seattle, WA

Morningstar Breakfast Muffins

Tested by
Chef Corso

2 - 4
servings

9
ingredients

10
minutes

**~4 oz /
~140 g**
per serving
+water

High Calorie

Low Water

9 Ingredients
◆ SPECIAL INGREDIENT

	US	METRIC
Powered Eggs/ Egg Substitute◆	4 TB	50 g
Water	4 TB	40 g
Cheese, your fav	4 oz	100 g
Tomato	1	1
Oil	2 TB	25 g
Morningstar sausage patties	8 oz	228 g
English muffins	4	4
Salt	to taste	to taste
Black Pepper	to taste	to taste
Total Weight	~1.3 lbs	~600 g

Steps
1. **Hydrate** eggs. **Sit** 5 min
2. **Slice** cheese, tomato
3. **TURN ON BURNER: MED HEAT**
4. **Add** oil
5. **Cook** patties. **Toast** muffs. **Reserve.**
6. **Add** eggs, seasoning. **Cook** 1-2 min
7. **Assemble** patties, eggs, tomatoes, cheese on muffs

EAT & PACK IT OUT

Did you know that?
The Yellowstone Caldera in Yellowstone National
Park is a super volcano that is responsible for
three of the world's six biggest volcano
eruptions.
Now you know!

Soyrizo Brekkie Burritos

Tested by
Bellolipop

2 - 4
servings

8
ingredients

25
minutes

**~5 oz /
~200 g**
per serving
+water

High Calorie

Vegetarian

Low Water

8 Ingredients

◆ SPECIAL INGREDIENT

	US	METRIC
Water	12 oz	100 g
Powdered Eggs ◆	4 TB	50 g
Salt	1/2 tsp	2 g
Soyrizo sausage ◆	13 oz	370 g
Cheese, your fav	4 oz	100 g
Avocado	2	2
Tortillas	4	4
Dehydrated Beans	1 C	95 g
Total Weight	~2 lbs	~900 kg

Steps

1. **Hydrate** eggs w/ 4 TB water, salt.
2. **Chop/Slice** soyrizo, cheese, avocado
3. **TURN ON BURNER: MED HEAT**
4. **Toast** tortillas. **Reserve**
5. **Add** soyrizo. **Cook** 2-3 min. **Stir**
6. **Add** remaining water. **Boil**
7. **Add** beans, eggs. **Stir**
8. **TURN OFF BURNER. Sit** 5-7 min to hydrate
9. **Stir**
10. **Layer** rizo mixture, cheese, avocado on tortillas
11. **Wrap**

EAT & PACK IT OUT

*Did you know that? Everglades National Park
protects more than 25% of Florida's original
everglades subtropical wetlands.
Now you know!*

Avocado, Tomato, Spinach Breakfast Sandwiches

Tested by
Chef Corso

2 - 4
servings

7
ingredients

20
minutes

**~6 oz /
~175 g**
per serving

Dairy Free

Vegan

Vegetarian

Gluten Free

Low Water

7 Ingredients

	US	METRIC
Olive Oil	2 TB	25 g
Bread Rolls	4	4
Avocado	1	1
Baby Tomatoes	1 pkg / 10.5 oz	285 g
Salt	1/2 tsp	2 g
Black Pepper	1/2 tsp	2 g
Spinach	6 oz	170 g
Total Weight	~1.5 lbs	~700 kg

Steps
1. **TURN ON BURNER: MED HEAT**
2. **Add** oil. **Toast** bread rolls. **Reserve**
3. **Slice** avocado
4. **Add** tomatoes, salt, pepper
5. **Cook** 2-4 min until burst
6. **Add** spinach. **Cook. Stir** until wilted
7. **Layer** tomato/spin mixture, avocado on rolls

EAT & PACK IT OUT

Did you know that? Utah's five national parks are all within easy driving distance of each other, which means that you can cross off five national parks from your "bucket list" on just one trip. Now you know!

AAAlmond Apricot Oatmeal

Tested by
Chef Corso

2
servings

6
ingredients

10
minutes

**~8 oz /
~230 g**

per serving
+water

Dairy Free

Vegan

Vegetarian

Gluten Free

6 Ingredients

	US	METRIC
Almond Milk	8 oz	225 g
Water	8 oz	225 g
Almonds	1/4 C	25 g
Apricots, dried	1/4 C	25 g
Instant Oatmeal	1 C	100 g
Almond Butter	1/4 C	25 g
Total Weight	~1.5 lbs	~700 g

Steps
1. **TURN ON BURNER: HIGH HEAT**
2. **Add** almond milk, water
3. **Boil**
4. **Chop** almonds, apricots
5. **Add** oatmeal
6. **Simmer** 3-5 min. **Stir**
7. **Add** almonds, apricots, almond butter. **Stir**

EAT & PACK IT OUT

Did you know that?
Great Smoky Mountains National Park is the
most visited national park in the USA.
Now you know!

Southwest Quinoa Bowl
Seattle, WA

Peanut Salad
Manzanar National
Historic Site
Independence, CA

Veggie Poke Bowl
Rocky Mountains, CO

Kashmir Cous Cous
Richmond, VA

Lunch

Seven Mile Creek Park
-Mankato, MN

Veggie Chop Suey

Tested by
CheezPleez

3 - 4
servings

8
ingredients

10
minutes

**~8 oz /
~230 g**
per serving

Dairy Free

Vegan

Vegetarian

Gluten Free

Low Water

8 ingredients

	US	METRIC
Red Pepper	1	1
Green Onions	1 bunch	1 bunch
Sesame Oil	2 TB	25 g
Shredded Carrots	5 oz	142 g
Snap Peas	8 oz	227 g
Bean Sprouts	12 oz	340 g
Soy Sauce	4 TB	50 g
Ginger Powder	2 tsp	5 g
Total Weight	~2 lbs	~1 kg

Steps
1. **Chop** red pepper into strips. **Chop** green onions
2. **TURN ON BURNER: HIGH HEAT**
3. **Add** sesame oil, carrots, red pepper, green onions, snap peas, bean sprouts
4. **Stir. Cook** 2-3 min
5. **Add** soy sauce, ginger powder
6. **Stir. Cook** 2-3 min

EAT & PACK IT OUT

*Did you know that? There are 15 species of
marmot and they have 4 toes on their front feet
and 5 on the their back feet.
Now you know!*

Southwest Quinoa Bowl

Tested by
Shushisnackin

2 – 4
servings

10
ingredients

15
minutes

**~10.5 oz /
~300 g**
per serving

High Calorie

Dairy Free

Vegan

Vegetarian

Gluten Free

No Burner

Low Water

10 Ingredients

◆ SPECIAL INGREDIENT	US	METRIC
Corn	1 ear	1 ear
Zucchini	1	1
Avocado	2	2
Black Beans	1 can/15 oz	425 g
Quinoa or grain mix, ◆ precooked	16 oz	440 g
Salt	1 tsp	5 g
Chili Flake or Hot Sauce	to taste	to taste
Lime	1	1
Cilantro	1/2 bunch	1/2 bunch
Olive Oil	1/4 C	50 g
Total Weight	~4.6 lbs	~1.2 kg

Steps

* NO BURNER RECIPE *

1. **Slice** corn off cob
2. **Chop** zucchini, avocado, cilantro, lime (wedges)
3. **Open** beans
4. **Add** all ingredients. **Squeeze** lime
5. **Mix. Sit** for 5-10 min

EAT & PACK IT OUT

Did you know that?
Corn, Beans and Squash are known as the
3 sisters in Mexican Cuisine.
All growing together in tasty harmony.
Now you now!

Kashmir Cous Cous

Tested by
RootsAreRad

2 - 4
servings

8
ingredients

10
minutes

**~5 oz /
~135 g**
per serving
+water

`Dairy Free`

`Vegan`

`Vegetarian`

8 Ingredients

	US	METRIC
Water	20 oz	600 ml
Cous Cous, instant	2 box/11.6 oz	2 box/320 g
Apricots, dried	1/2 C	50 g
Dates, pitted	1/2 C	50 g
Almonds, chopped	1/2 C	50 g
Indian Curry Spice Mix	1 TB	10 g
Salt	1/2 tsp	2 g
Lemon or	1/2	1/2
Apple Cider Vinegar	1 TB	12 g
Total Weight	~2.5 lbs	~1.1 kg

Steps
1. **TURN ON BURNER: HIGH HEAT**
2. **Boil** water
3. **Add** cous cous. **Stir. Sit** for 5-10 min
4. **Chop** apricots, dates, almonds
5. When cous cous is done, **Add** apricots, dates, almonds, spice mix, salt (if no salt in mix)
6. **Mix**
7. **Add** juice of half lemon/vinegar

EAT & PACK IT OUT

Did you know that?
Cous cous is actually a pasta, a really small one.
A combo of water and usually semolina flour.
Now you know!

Peanut Salad

Tested by
MangoMango

2 - 3
servings

9
ingredients

20
minutes

**~9 oz /
~260 g**
per serving
+water

Dairy Free

Vegan

Vegetarian

Gluten Free

No Burner

Low Water

9 ingredients

	US	METRIC
Red Pepper	1	1
Kale/Spinach/ Collard Greens	1/2 bunch / 4 stalks	100 g
Black Eyed Peas	1 can/pouch /15 oz	425 g
Peanuts	1/2 C	75 g
Apple Cider Vinegar	2 TB	35 g
Olive Oil	2 TB	35 g
Garlic Powder	1 tsp	5 g
Salt	to taste	to taste
Hot Sauce/Cayenne Pepper	to taste	to taste
Total Weight	~1.8 lbs	~775 g

Steps

No Cook/No Burner Recipe

1. **Chop** red pepper, kale
2. **Open** can/pouch black eyed peas. **Drain**
3. **Combine** all ingredients
4. **Sit** for 10 min

EAT & PACK IT OUT

*If you can't find black eyed peas,
chickpeas/garbanzo beans can work as well.*

Veggie Poke Bowl

Tested by
followyourownpath

2 - 4
servings

10
ingredients

15
minutes

**~12 oz /
~325 g**

per serving
+water

Dairy Free

Vegan

Vegetarian

Gluten Free

10 ingredients

◆ SPECIAL INGREDIENT	US	METRIC
Water	16 oz	500 ml
Instant Rice	2 C	370 g
Snap Peas	8 oz	225 g
Cucumber	1	1
Avocado	2	2
Rice Vinegar	2 TB	25 g
Pickled Ginger ◆	6 oz	160 g
Edamame, shelled	8 oz	225 g
Sesame Seeds	2 TB	18 g
Soy Sauce	4 TB	50 g
Total Weight	~4 lbs	~1.8 kg

Steps

1. **TURN ON BURNER: HIGH HEAT**
2. **Add** water. **Boil**
3. **Add** rice. **Stir. Cover. Let sit** for 5 min
4. **TURN OFF BURNER**
5. **Chop** snap peas, cucumber, avocado
6. **Add** rice vinegar to rice. **Stir**
7. **Add** vegetables to rice. **Stir**
8. **Garnish** w/ sesame seeds, soy sauce

EAT & PACK IT OUT

Great with some sriracha or spicy mayo!

Warm Asian Pasta Salad

Tested by
Chef Corso

1-2
servings

8
ingredients

10
minutes

**~5 oz /
~150 g**
per serving
+water

8 Ingredients

	US	METRIC
Water	8 oz	250 ml
Orzo Pasta	4 oz	100 g
Soy Sauce Packets	1-2	1-2
Oil	2 tsp	10 g
Rice Vinegar	1-2 tsp	10 g
Wasabi Peas	3 TB	45 g
Shredded Carrots	1/4 C	60 g
Sesame Sticks/Snaps	1/4 C	60 g
Total Weight	~1.2 lbs	~550 g

Steps
1. **TURN ON BURNER: HEAT HEAT**
2. **Add** water. **Boil**
3. **Add** pasta. **Boil** until soft. **Drain**
4. **TURN OFF BURNER**
5. **Add** rest of ingredients and mix

EAT & PACK IT OUT

Notes:
*Green onion, ginger powder or sesame seeds
would be great too!*

White Bean & Kale Soup
Theseus Lake, WA

**Lasagna w/
"meat" sauce**
Portland, OR

**Sweet Potato
Black Bean Chili**
Tacoma, WA

Tamale Bowl
Seattle, WA

Dinner

Northeast Coast, USA

#TheStew

Tested by
Yun

2 - 4
servings

10
ingredients

20
minutes

**~ 4.5 oz /
~125 g**
per serving
+water

High Calorie

Dairy Free

Vegan

Vegetarian

Gluten Free

10 ingredients

◆ SPECIAL INGREDIENT	US	METRIC
Kale, Beet or Chard greens	1-2 C	200 g
Water	32 oz	1 L
Chickpeas, Dehydrated ◆	2 C	215 g
Coconut Milk Powder ◆	1/4 C	30 g
Ground Ginger	2 tsp	10 g
Ground Turmeric	2 tsp	10 g
Salt	1 tsp	5 g
Garlic Powder	1 tsp	5 g
Chili Flake	1/2 tsp	2 g
Sumac ◆	1 tsp	2 g
Total Weight	~3.3 lbs	~1.5 kg

Steps
1. **Chop/Rip** greens
2. **TURN ON BURNER: HIGH HEAT**
3. **Add** all ingredients except sumac
4. **Stir. Boil. Cook** 5-10 min until chickpeas soft
5. **Sprinkle** sumac

EAT & PACK IT OUT

*Did you know that? This is a take on New York
Times food writer Alison Roman's "The Stew."
You can eat this classic on a mountain top!
Now you know!*

White Bean & Kale Soup

Tested by
Bellolipop

2 – 4
servings

10
ingredients

25
minutes

**~6.5 oz /
~175 g**

per serving
+water

Dairy Free

Vegan

Vegetarian

Gluten Free

10 ingredients

◆ SPECIAL INGREDIENT

	US	METRIC
Kale	1 bunch	1 bunch
Carrot	2-3	2-3
Shallot	2	2
Lemon	1	1
Olive Oil	2 TB	25 g
Garlic Powder	1/2 tsp	2 g
Salt	1 tsp	5 g
Black Pepper	1/2 tsp	2 g
White Beans, dehydrated ◆	1 C	140 g
(or other legumes)		
Water	16 oz	500 ml
Total Weight	~2.6 lbs	~1.2 kg

Steps

1. **Chop** kale, carrot, shallot
2. **Cut** lemon wedges
3. **TURN ON BURNER: HIGH HEAT**
4. **Add** olive oil, vegetables, garlic, salt, pepper
5. **Cook** 5 min. **Stir**
6. **Add** white beans, water
7. **Cook** 5-10 min
8. **Garnish** w/ lemon wedges

EAT & PACK IT OUT

*Try some other root veggies or switch out the
beans for potatoes.
Canned beans work great as well!*

Sweet Potato Black Bean Chili

Tested by
Chef Corso

2 - 4
servings

10
ingredients

30
minutes

**~13 oz /
~360 g**
per serving
+water

High Calorie

Dairy Free

Vegan

Vegetarian

Gluten Free

Low Water

10 ingredients

	US	METRIC
Sweet Potato / Yam	1	1
Shallot	2	2
Red Bell Pepper	1	1
Black Beans or	2 cans (31 oz total) /	2 cans (880g) /
Dehydrated Beans	2 C	50 g
Olive Oil	2 TB	25 g
Tomato Paste	2 oz	25 g
Chili Powder	2 TB	30 g
Water	8 oz	250 ml
Salt	1 tsp	5 g
Avocado	1	1
Total Weight	~3.7 lbs	~1.7 kg

Steps
1. **Chop** sweet potato, shallot, bell pepper
2. **Open** black beans
3. **TURN ON BURNER: MED HEAT**
4. **Add** olive oil, vegetables. **Cook** 3-5 min
5. **Add** tomato paste. **Stir**
6. **Add** black beans, chili powder, water, salt
7. **Boil. Cook** 10 min or until sweet potatoes done
8. **Slice** avocado. **Add**

EAT & PACK IT OUT

*Did you know that? The moose is the largest
member of the deer family.
Now you know!*

Lasagna w/ "Meat" Sauce

Tested by
Red Beard

2 - 4
servings

10
ingredients

25
minutes

**~6 oz /
~150 g**
per serving
+water

High Calorie

Vegan

Vegetarian

10 ingredients

	US	METRIC
Water	32 oz	1 L
Lasagna Noodles, any	1/2 LB	225 g
Garlic / Garlic Powder	2 clvs / 1/2 tsp	2 clvs / 2 g
Field Roast or other fake meat	5 oz	140 g
Olive Oil	2 TB	25 g
Tomato Paste	1 Tube / 4.5 oz	125 g
Italian Seasoning, dried	1 TB	10 g
Chili Flake	1 tsp	5 g
Salt	1 tsp	5 g
optional Parmesan Cheese	2 oz	50 g
Total Weight	~3.5 lbs	~1.6 kg

Steps

1. **TURN ON BURNER: HIGH HEAT**
2. **Add** water, pasta
3. **Boil** pasta until soft. **Reserve** 8 oz water in pot
4. **Chop** garlic, field roast.
5. **Add** olive oil, tomato paste, field roast, garlic, seasoning, chili flake, salt
6. **Stir, stir. Cook** 2-5 min
7. **Garnish** w/ parmesan cheese

EAT & PACK IT OUT

Did you know that? There are over 10,000 varieties of tomato. They come in a variety of colors including pink, purple, black, yellow and white.
Now you know!

Tamale Bowl

Tested by
WorldSpiceMerchants

2 - 4
servings

10
ingredients

20
minutes

**~6 oz /
~150 g**
per serving
+water

High Calorie

Vegetarian

Gluten Free

10 ingredients

	US	METRIC
Shallot	2	2
Red Pepper	1	1
Oil	2 TB	50 g
Polenta/Grits/Masa	1 C	90 g
Water	24 oz	700 ml
Salt	1 tsp	5 g
Chili Powder Spice Mix	2 TB	25 g
Avocado	1	1
Lime	1	1
Queso Fresco/Feta	2 oz	50 g
Total Weight	~3 lbs	~1.3 kg

Steps

1. **Chop** shallot, red pepper
2. **TURN ON BURNER: MED HEAT**
3. **Add** oil, shallot, pepper. **Stir**
4. **Cook** 2 min
5. **Add** polenta, water, salt, chili powder. **Stir**
6. **TURN BURNER TO LOW**
7. **Stir. Simmer** 5-7 min until cooked
8. **Garnish** w/ avocado, lime wedge and queso fresco

EAT & PACK IT OUT

Did you know that?
Corn is grown on every continent except
Antarctica.
Now you know!

Swimming Rama

Tested by
eliamoves

2 - 4
servings

9
ingredients

15
minutes

**~8 oz /
~250 g**
per serving
+water

High Calorie

Dairy Free

Vegan

Vegetarian

Gluten Free

Low Water

9 ingredients

	US	METRIC
Tofu / Packaged Chicken	10 oz	300 g
Lime	1	1
Sesame Oil	2 TB	25 g
Nut Butter, your fav	1 C	250 g
Rice Vinegar	2 TB	25 g
Sriracha Sauce	2 TB	25 g
Fish Sauce / Salt	1 tsp	5 g
Water	2 oz	60 g
Spinach	10 oz bag	284 g
Total Weight	~2.2 lbs	~1 kg

Steps
1. **Chop** Tofu. **Cut** lime
2. **TURN ON BURNER: MED HEAT**
3. **Add** oil, nut butter, vinegar, sriracha, fish sauce/salt, water
4. **Cook** 2-3 min. **Stir, stir**
5. **Add** tofu/chicken
6. **Cook** 1-2 min. **Stir**
7. **Add** spinach
8. **Cook** 1-2 min until wilted. **Stir**

EAT & PACK IT OUT

Add some rice or rice noodles on the side!

Blueberry Banana Crisp
Lake Crescent, WA

**Chili Lime
Spiced Popcorn**
Lake Washington, WA

**Pineapple
Upside-Down Bowl**
Germantown
Metro Park, OH

Boca Spiced Nuts
Port Angeles, WA

Dessert/ Snacks

Lake Crescent, WA

Blueberry Banana Crisp

Tested by
Mr. Preacher

2
servings

4
ingredients

10
minutes

**~8 oz /
~220 g**
per serving
+water

Dairy Free

Vegan

Vegetarian

Gluten Free

Low Water

4 ingredients

	US	METRIC
Banana Chips	3/4 C	75 g
Blueberries, fresh or dry	6 oz/4 oz	170 g/50 g
Water	4 oz	125 ml
Granola, your fav	1 C	140 g
Total Weight	~1.25 lbs	~560 g

Steps
1. **TURN ON BURNER: MED HEAT**
2. **Add** banana chips, blueberries, water
3. **Stir. Cook** until hydrated. 3-5 min.
4. **TURN OFF BURNER**
5. **Add** granola
6. **Stir**

EAT & PACK IT OUT

Notes:
Great with a squeeze of lemon or jazz it up with
some cinnamon, nutmeg or allspice!

Pineapple Upside-Down Bowl

Tested by
ravoneous.on.the.trail

2 - 4
servings

6
ingredients

10
minutes

**~3.5 oz /
~100 g**
per serving
+water

6 ingredients

	US	METRIC
Pineapple, dried	1/2 C	100 g
Cherries, dried	1/4 C	50 g
Water	2 oz	60 ml
Brown Sugar	1 TB	12 g
Oil	2 TB	30 g
Graham Crackers	5-7 oz	200 g
Total Weight	~1 lb	~450 g

Steps
1. **Chop/Rip** pineapple, if needed
2. **TURN ON BURNER: MED HEAT**
3. **Add** all except graham. **Stir**
4. **Cook** until fruit softens
5. **Crush** crackers
6. **Add** crackers. **Stir**

EAT & PACK IT OUT

*Did you know that? This pineapple upside down
cake was a winner of a contest put on by the
Hawaiian Pineapple Company in 1925.
Now you know!*

Chili Lime Spiced Popcorn

Tested by
Chef Corso

4 - 6
servings

5
ingredients

10
minutes

**~1.3 oz /
~33 g**
per serving

Dairy Free

Vegan

Vegetarian

Gluten Free

Low Water

5 ingredients

	US	METRIC
Oil	3 TB	40 g
Popcorn	2 oz	55 g
Salt	1 tsp	5 g
Chili Powder	2 TB	35 g
Lime	1	1
Total Weight	~8 oz	~200 g

Steps
1. **Cut** lime
2. **TURN ON BURNER: HIGH HEAT**
3. **Add** oil & 3 kernels
4. **WAIT** for kernels to pop!
5. **Add** all kernels, salt, chili powder
6. **Cover. Move quick! Toss, toss**
7. When done popping, **Add** lime squeeze
8. **Toss**

EAT & PACK IT OUT

*Make sure to cover while you toss or you will get
splattered with oil! No bueno.*

Boca Spiced Nuts

Tested by
KaiserWilhelmNH

2 - 3
servings

7
ingredients

5
minutes

**~2 oz /
~40 g**
per serving
+water

High Calorie

Dairy Free

Vegan

Vegetarian

Gluten Free

Low Water

7 ingredients

◆ SPECIAL INGREDIENT	US	METRIC
Oil	1 TB	15 g
Mixed Nuts	1 C	100 g
Salt	to taste	to taste
Smoked Paprika ◆	2 tsp	10 g
Garlic Powder	1/2 tsp	2 g
Sugar Packet	2	2
Sumac ◆	1/2 tsp	2 g
Total Weight	~5 oz	~130 g

Steps
1. **TURN ON BURNER: LOW HEAT**
2. **Add** oil, nuts. **Stir**
3. **Cook** 1-2 min until lightly toasted
4. **Add** seasonings, sugar. **Stir**
5. **Cook** 1 min until coated

EAT & PACK IT OUT

This is a great recipe to spice up those boring nut mixes. Also great with something a little spicy. Go nuts!

Get out there...

...and COOK!

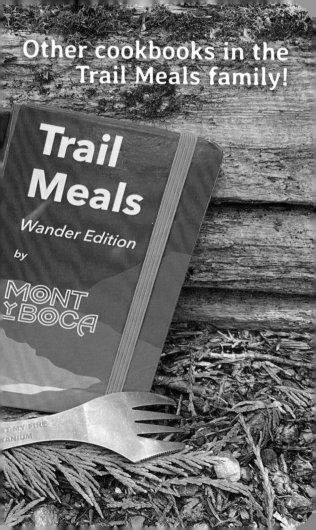

Other cookbooks in the Trail Meals family!

About the Chef

Chef Corso likes to eat and go outside. He's also a classically trained chef, training in Napa Valley and Northern Italy. On his treks, he noticed the food options were a little lacking. They were dry, salty, expensive and out of a bag. He started testing simple recipes using fresh ingredients, all with the hiker/camper in mind.

The results were amazing! Tasty food that complimented the beautiful vista like nothing he had experienced before. It's his goal to share these recipes as he believes everyone should eat well on their outdoor adventures. Outdoor Eats can show you how.

Get outside. Eat well. Share the tasty experience.

While Outdoor Eats is headquartered in Seattle, Washington, all recipes are trail-tested around the world.

BocaBoca

Chef Corso

Follow along:
www.outdooreats.com
Instagram/Facebook/TikTok:
@outdooreats365
YouTube: Chef Corso

Credits:
Photography: Outdoor Eats, Sattva Photography
Cover Art: Ronald Viernes, Makoto Sebuchi
Logo: Stephanie Jung
Cookbook Formatting: Makoto Sebuchi
Editors: Sarah Warren, Paul Stanley, R.D. Saathoff
Third Edition - Trail Meals - Terra Edition
ISBN 978-1-7341902-2-9
Get outside. Eat well. Share the tasty experience.
#elevateyourmeals
bocaboca